DROPPING THE BOW

DROPPING THE BOW

Poems from Ancient India

Translated by
Andrew Schelling

Companions for the Journey Series: Volume 15

WHITE PINE PRESS / BUFFALO, NEW YORK

This book was originally published in 1991 by John Ellison and Leslie Link's Broken Moon Press. Seven poems had appeared in a letterpress chapbook, *Claw Moraine*, hand produced by David Sheidlower at Coincidence Press. In 2003 Bob and Susan Arnold's longhouse produced a chaplet, "Poems from the Sattasai of King Hala," containing twelve of the poems I've added to the current edition. My gratitude goes to these folk, as well as to the editors of *Bombay Gin, Chicago Review, lift, Kyoto Review, Moe's Books Broadsides, Ploughshares, Stone Bridge*, and *Yellow Silk*, who published many when I first sent them out.

Publication of this book was made possible, in part, by funding from the National Endowment for the Arts, which believes that a great country deserves great art, and with public funds from the New York State Council on the Arts, a State Agency.

Printed and bound in the United States of America.

First Edition

Cover image: Detail from "Todi Ragini," Indian, Rajasthari. About 1760. Used by permission of the Museum of Fine Arts, Boston.

Library of Congress Control Number: 2008921649

ISBN: 978-1-893996-92-2

White Pine Press
P.O. Box 236
Buffalo, New York 14201
www.whitepine.org

To the memory of Cid Corman

शरदिन्दुसुन्दरुचिश्चेतसि सा मे गिरां देवी ।
अपहृत्य तमः संततमर्थानखिलान्प्रकाशयतु ॥

Shining with the luster
of moon in autumn
may She, goddess Language,
stripping from my
heart the endless woven darkness,
cast the nature of all
things into light.

—Vishvanatha

Contents

Preface to the Second Edition

9

Poems from the Sanskrit

15

Poems from *King Hala's Gaha-kosa* or *Book of Songs*

69

Afterword

101

Notes on the Poets & Poems

111

Bibliography

123

Preface to the Second Edition

In the mid-nineteenth century Henry David Thoreau may have owned the single largest collection of Sanskrit books in the Western Hemisphere. A British friend and admirer, Thomas Cholmondeley, had a life-altering visit to Thoreau in Concord. On his return home he rounded up what books of the East he could find in London and shipped them across the Atlantic in gratitude. Thoreau built a bookcase in his bedroom, proudly displaying the volumes to visitors. He never bothered to learn the language. When a friend asked why, Thoreau replied that for all he knew he had the world's wisdom by his bed-stand. What if he learnt to read them? He might discover all he owned was a rack of old books.

Since at least Thoreau's day, North Americans have been fascinated with India's spiritual traditions, her mythologies, the poetry of excruciating desire, the intricate music, colorful folk arts, medicine, cuisine, and glittering metaphysics. Anyone who hopes to consult the original languages, though, finds the resources frustratingly limited. Living in Colorado as I do, if I want to dig into the actual texts I have to travel a distance about the width of India. Few workable libraries of Sanskrit deep enough for research have been built anywhere in North America.

The Sanskrit language has been my Concord River. Thoreau called his the Musketaquid, or Grass-ground River, giving it back its native name. That's where he set down his canoe. The place I set mine down, for this, my first book, was the library at U.C. Berkeley. There I located the texts that gave me India's old poems.

The poetry collected in *Dropping the Bow* belongs to a tradition that emerged two thousand years ago, in watersheds drained by other rivers, the Narmada and Godavari. The general term for these lyrics in Sanskrit is *kavya,* a word that means poetry, in a high art sense. This distinguishes the artistic tradition from the more ordinary task of coining verses. For many preliterate cultures, committing information to verse is the handiest way to store it. India excelled at this. Treatises on philosophy, medicine, warfare, ritual, music, architecture, table manners, bedroom manners, even mathematics, got put to verse. Rhythmic pattern, magical figures of speech, compressed forms of expression, and tiny syllabic codes were all used to keep things in memory.

Poetry is something else. Its origin in India, as in many places, lies in song.

The first book to discuss poetry, the *Natya Shastra* (ca. 400 BCE-200 CE) attributed to Bharata Muni, describes an old form of theater from which poetry arose. Standard Sanskrit poetic meters carry names like "Tiger's Play" and "Girl with a Ball," which immediately conjure dance steps, masks, costumes. Yet poetry and song don't need stages, costumes, orchestras, or dancers. They are the most portable of arts. I don't think I'm imagining it when I detect traces of hunting and fertility magic in the erotic poems of classical India, which could stretch back to the last Ice Age.

Here I want to point out that the bulk of the poems are love songs. Their eroticism is playful and heartbreaking, and utterly refined.

Since the time of the *Natya Shastra*, the key concept in Sanskrit poetry has been *rasa*. It is an archaic word that meant sap, juice, fluid, semen. "Spirit juice," Cid Corman once called it in a letter, "the juice of life." Later, *rasa* came to mean essence, flavor, the core of experience; and eventually, the permanent emotions that bring a work of art to life. Poets recognized eight *rasas*: erotic, comic, grievous, angry, heroic, fearsome, odious, marvelous. A good poet worked them all, and I think all emerge in this book. But Indian poets never wavered from a belief that the erotic—*sringara*—was the most primal. Love: learned in the cradle of family, the way language is learned at your mother's breast.

Much surviving Sanskrit poetry comes to the contemporary world in large, well-organized anthologies. These contain chapters covering the seasons, love, grief, kings and poor people, the sun, the moon, old age and cremation, and dozens of other topics. I've drawn many of these poems from the *Subhasita-ratna-kosa*, a collection compiled between 1100 and 1130 by a Buddhist abbot of Jagaddala college in Bengal, named Vidyakara. I have found other poems in a range of other surviving collections. In particular, there are the poems from King Hala's *Gaha-kosa* or *Book of Songs*. Fortunately several editions of this 2000 year old anthology survive.

✳

I want to acknowledge several debts. First, to Cid Corman. I began corresponding with Cid in 1984. In 1989 when I gathered these translations, I sent them to Kyoto for his comments. In a characteristic act of generosity towards a young poet with no published books, he combed through the manuscript, making numerous suggestions. He also sent a list of possible titles. *Dropping the Bow* I liked best—partly because the poem he drew it from is one of the most memorable I have seen anywhere. The title catches the archaic magic associated with the hunter's bow, and echoes poet Robert Duncan's *Bending the Bow,* a book I have treasured, argued with, and studied for years.

John Ellison and Leslie Link of Broken Moon Press took a chance with the manuscript. At the time India's poetry was scarcely known in North America (it is only slightly better known today). They brought out the first edition in 1991, and the New York based Academy of American Poets, described by Wikipedia as the "preeminent organization in the United States dedicated to the art of poetry," awarded *Dropping the Bow* their prize for translation in 1992. It was the first time a book of Asia's poetry had received the prestigious award.

I did the translations for this book over a stretch of ten or twelve years. I was living in Northern California at the time, on a flank of the Coast Range that looks over the Pacific, toward Asia. On that slope, where "the world behind will watch us endure prophetical things" (Robinson Jeffers), Asia seemed remarkably close. In New York, I suppose, Asia looked pretty far out, culturally. My gratitude goes to Edmund Keeley for choosing this book for the Academy's award. Equally it goes to the musicians, artists, scholars, philosophers, and rickshaw drivers of India, who pointed me toward Sanskrit in the first place. In their honor I have added seventeen new poems and notes on the poets.

Fourth of July Valley, Colorado
June 2007

Poems from the Sanskrit

Having silenced the silver
chains at my ankles,
bound up the noisy
jewels on my waistband,
and watched the nearby
households go to sleep—
Fate, why are you angry?
I'd just set forth
when you spurred the cold
new-risen moon, bright
as a Kashmiri girl's breast,
over the open road.

Anonymous

Her quick eyes
and animated mouth
unsettle me.
So, of course,
her lifted breasts,
full lips—
soft fruits of desire.
But why should a
single wisp of hair,
stroked beneath her
navel like
some unforgettable
line of poetry,
reduce me to such
anguish?

Bhartrihari

I know
I was trembling
ivy.
He gripped me,
stroked my breasts
freely,
stole his hands
down past my ribcage—
this much
I remember but then
my resolve broke,
the shaking stopped,
I don't know
what to think.

Anonymous

How resplendent
she looks
threshing the winter rice!
Each time she lifts
her arms her bracelets
chatter together
and the necklace of stones
swings from her chest.
Again and again
she raises the shining paddle—
at each effort
her blouse slips back
exposing a fresh
line of fingernail marks
next to her breast.

Vagura

Next morning
when a damnfool parrot—
right before her parents—
starts to mimic
last night's cries of love,
the girl leaps up,
blushing,
claps her hands to
start the children dancing—
jangle of her bracelets
drowning out
the parrot's calls.

Anonymous

Friend,
the lamp flame was flaring
into night's darkest
corners. My lover,
an adept in the flavors
of love,
made slow
very slow love
because the bed
grates like a talkative
neighbor.

Anonymous

Words of a Go-Between

And one other thing—
don't be afraid
this girl being slender is fragile—
you've seen bees
drop into the mango blossom,
has a stem ever snapped?
Take her firmly.
Hesitant pressing
never extracted
the sugarcane's sap.

Anonymous

Unable to cast
a semblance
of my girl's face, her dark eyes,
no doubt the moon
is reshaping its cold
disc, only
again to dissolve it.

Anonymous

No one visible up ahead,
no one approaches
from behind.
Not a footprint on the road.
Am I alone?
This much is clear—
the path the ancient
poets opened
is choked with brush,
and I've long since left
the public thoroughfare.

Dharmakirti

Shamelessly
orange like a
parrot's beak,
arousing with a lover's
touch the clustered
lotus buds,
I praise this
great wheel the sun—
rising it is an
earring for
the Lady of the East.

Vidya

Water drops glint from her
wildly tossed curls.
She crosses her wrists
gathering the new luxuriant weight
of her breasts.
Thighs wet & translucent with silk
bent a bit forward—
nervously eyeing the
bank-side thickets she steps
from the creek.

Bhojadeva

This time let me
be the lady
you play the lover—

to which the girl
protests
shaking her head

but eyes
wide like a
deer's eyes she threads
a bracelet onto
his wrist.

Anonymous

I've never fastened
a bracelet
white like the autumn
moon's light
to my wrist.
Nor have I tasted
the pliant lip of a
young wife, trembling
with uncertainty.
I obtained no
renown in the places
the gods inhabit,
by knowledge
or by swordsmanship,
but spent my bitter days
in a college
classroom, among the
noisy, impudent
students.

Anonymous

Slim-waisted friend,
look—
spreading its arch
over Love's
phantom city,
the faint crescent moon—
where the separate
gazes of lovers
parted to separate
countries meet.

Rajashekhara

For a moment
it reaches out waking
then gutters
again in the dark—
the mind of an old man,
the flame
of a lamp burning out.

Anonymous

Little gasps
of breath,
her eyelids barely parted,
bristling skin
and beads of sweat—

above love's temple waves
love's banner,
and I
can only bow my head
at the mysterious change
a woman
undergoes—

Anonymous

Through tears
she saw mist
and the clustering
rainclouds. "If you leave…"
her voice trailed and she
clung to my jacket,
scuffing the ground
where she dug in.
What she then did
no poet's
words command
the power to tell.

from the *Amarushataka*

Considering many
things in my heart
I hang onto life.
Don't you succumb to
bewilderment now,
lovely one. Whose
lot is just
joy or just sorrow?
Fortune goes down
and goes up like a
cartwheel revolving.

Kalidasa, from the *Meghaduta*

A snatch of dream,
a juggler's contrivance—
making love to her
lasts a flickering instant,
then disillusion.
A hundred times
I tell myself this
but still can't forget
those antelope eyes.

Dharmakirti

Rain slants steadily
through the night-bound
toddy-palm forest.
Concealed by huge fronds
the elephants,
eyes half open,
ears beating a slow rhythm and trunks
slung over their tusk-tips,
listen to the unbroken
downpour.

Hastipaka

They seize one's heart
these rice-husking
songs of the women—
bracelets chiming
along their bare arms
as they swing
the glistening rice paddles.
Teasing, tender,
now teasing again—
a low-toned *hum*
forced by exertion from
swaying breasts
underlies the singing
like a drone.

Yogeshvara

Once again
you mount this playful
woman's breasts and touch
the tender region
along her thighs.
Closing one arm around you
she draws forth
your pleasure
with measured strokes
of her hand.
Some other lifetime
what austerities
did you practice, O sitar,
to win this reward?

Vacaspati

Praises!
the man-lion claws
of the god
that tore the demon-king's
belly to shreds—
remembering which
the demons,
even when screwing,
shudder beneath the fingernails
of their women.

Anonymous

Her skirt
spattered with gore,
buffalo demon
skewed
on her pike,
Gauri the goddess
as if flowered
with menses,
is shamed—
is laughed on by gods—
        —is victorious!

Gonanda

Neighbor, please
keep an eye on my house
for a moment.
The baby's father
finds our well-water
tasteless, and refuses
to drink it. I'd better
go, though alone,
down to the river,
though the thick
tamala trees and stands
of broken cane
are likely to
scratch my breasts.

Vidya

Dense downhanging branches,
shade on the riverbank,
dew on the wind—
O Murala River—
clear sand,
whistling waterbirds,
who made your
willows such refuge,
a married woman could
come here for love,
undetected...

Vidya

A south wind stirs
languidly now
loosening the resolute
pride of these women. Scented
with camphor it sports
across the ocean and deeply
agitates their wombs.

Anonymous

Last year and each
year before,
birdsong and spiced wind
blew down from the
Kerala hills.
But restless, unbridled,
my wits, friend,
have never been
so distracted as this year.

Utpalaraja

On makeshift
bedding in the cucumber
garden,
the hilltribe girl
clings to her
exhausted lover.
Limbs still chafing
with pleasure, dissolving
against him she
now and again with
one bare foot
jostles a shell necklace
that hangs from a
vine on the fence—
rattling it
through the night,
scaring the jackals off.

Vidya

Don't go!
brings bad luck.
Leave! is an oily
word and sounds hollow.
Stay! just a futile command.
Do what you like,
pretends I'm indifferent
but, *I can't live without you,*
really doesn't apply.
What should I say
when you pull on your trousers
and get up to leave?

Anonymous

Get away
from the riverbank, boy!
Why do you
stare while I'm bathing?
This is no place
to frequent
if you live in fear
of your wife.

from the *Dhvanyaloka*

You hold the bankroll,
but words
speed to my command,
just like this!
What you want
you get by force—
I speak
and cut pride
where it sits in a man's eye.
Mad for a few dollars
people debase themselves
to you, but they
come hear me dispel
their mental phlegm.
You don't give a
damn for your poets, King—
less even than we care
for you—so I'll leave.

Bhartrihari

Fate is a cruel
and proficient potter,
my friend. Forcibly
spinning the wheel
of anxiety, he lifts misfortune
like a cutting tool. Now
having kneaded my heart
like a lump of clay,
he lays it on his
wheel and gives a spin.
What he intends to produce
I cannot tell.

Vidya

Why spread stories
about somebody's girlfriend?
But a gossip
by nature,
southern by birth,
I can't hold my tongue.
In that house, in this house,
at the markets and crossroads,
inside the taverns—
that lady you're
sleeping with, sir,
she canters about like a
bitch in heat. And hah—!
she's called Fame.

Vidya

Even without make-up
your face has that blue
luster our forest
flowers are known for.
Cosmetics add nothing.
How can you ornament
what by its own
nature is beautiful?

Bhamaha

Scarlet betel-nut juice
spattered about,
aloe paste
dashed here and there
in yellow streaks.
Richer stains—impressions
of sandalwood oil,
red footprints
from the rouge on her feet.
Petals that
clung to her hair
have dropped in the
scattered folds—
every position
a woman took pleasure from
is told on these bedsheets.

from the *Amarushataka*

Some indeterminate
thing of no pleasure,
no pain,
transcending description,
respectable minds have declared
"such is release."

But this
trembling girl,
hair on her
arms and legs thrilling,
a glint in her eye
as though she'd had liquor—

the skirt when it slips from
her figure
to my mind this
is release.

from the *Shringaratilaka*, attributed to *Kalidasa*

Now that the rainy
season is on us,
restless wild mountain tribe couples
no longer descend
the paths to make love here.
The bamboo thickets
flanking these hillside
creeks have grown quiet.
Along the banks, fresh
shoots are emerging,
tips clad in soft bark,
black as the skin
on a kid-goat's ear.

Anonymous

Her girlfriends in the morning
press her for details
of the night.
She averts her face—
a bud unopened gives no scent.
But as they ornament
her breasts with lines
of musk and saffron,
involuntary shudders
disclose the unseen nailmarks.

Murari

To His Prince

Your enemy's son
weeps and rages
when the wild forest peacocks
though called by household
names do not respond.
But your enemy's
wife, her crying
is almost inaudible.

Yogeshvara

The tribesmen dispatch
creature after
living creature to Durga,
Goddess who dwells in a craggy wilderness grotto.
They slosh the blood on a field-spirit tree.
Then joined by their women at dusk
go wild to the gourd-lute
stopping just to pass liquor around—
the old way—
in a *bilva* fruit husk.

Yogeshvara

The curse upon me ends
when Vishnu
rises from his serpent bed.
Close your eyes, let
the four remaining months
drift past. Then
all those desires
ripened by separation
we'll slake at night
beneath the huge harvest moon.

Kalidasa, from the *Meghaduta*

Don't say
a single word of me
or reproach him
for taking his time,
        just say

I hope the wind
off Malabar
hasn't reached you
I hope the mango tree's
not bloomed.

Vakkuta

Quickly, in secret,
protecting the girl
whose lover has
left her, friends
snip the buds
as they appear
on the jasmine.

Rajashekhara

The gold of poetry
gets smelted and refined
from the speech of
unreflective men.
Let us go
cheerfully among them
with poised minds.

Varahamihira

Dark clouds
mount the directions,
the sky
seems tossed
with flame and vapor.
Dark earth
presses white blossoms
out of the tangled grass.
Time now
to draw close,
talk, eat, make love.
Whoever's lover
has left her
goes to the pavilion
of Death.

Vidya

Set beside a
fawn-eyed girl, wilted
from hours of loving,
the world itself seems worthless.
When her partner
flings the bedsheets back
eyes absorbed
by what others never glimpse,
her hands flee to her
thighs, her breasts,
then to her
lover's eyes.

Anonymous

What wealth,
that you can chatter
about a night spent
with your lover—
the teasings,
smiles, whispered words—
even his special smell.
Because, O my friends I swear—
from the moment
my lover's hand touched
my skirt, I remember
nothing at all.

Vidya

Unclasp your arms.
Get up and leave this man,
you've worn him out
with a night of loving.
Dawn is reddening, girl,
you can hear the wild cocks calling
from house to house.

Patanjali

The man who first
took my flower's
still with me.
The moon-drenched nights have returned.
Fresh jasmine blows in from
the Vindhya Range
and the girl is still me.
But her heart?
It grieves for those nights
we stole off to the riverbank
and made love in the
cane groves
forever.

Shilabhattarika

Critics scoff
at my work
and declare their contempt—
no doubt they've got
their own little wisdom.
I write nothing for them.
But because time is
endless and our planet
vast, I write these
poems for a person
who will one day be born
with my sort of heart.

Bhavabhuti

And what of those
arbors of vines
that grow where the river
drops away from Kalinda Mountain?
They conspired in the love
games of herding girls
and watched over the veiled
affairs of Radha.
Now that the days
are gone when I cut their
tendrils, and laid them
down for couches of love,
I wonder if they've
grown brittle and if
their splendid blue flowers
have dried up.

Vidya

Poems from King Hala's Gaha-kosa
or Book of Songs

Sneering
lady of the big house
scatters straw—
a bed for the traveler—
at dawn gathers it
in her arms
crying

Anonymous

All day
dragging a plough
through tough thick mud
in bed he's
feeble and sleeps—
while one more night
not fucked
his young wife lies there
cursing the months
of rain

Anonymous

Crying
she heaps up
the last
madhuka flowers—
painful to look at—
as if from
the burning ground
gathering
bones

Shribala

Only
the swollen waters
of Godavari River
and the nights and midnights of rain
have seen
his good luck
and my
unladylike
daring

Makaradhvaja

Festival day
her lover
whispers the wrong name—
now her jewelry
weighs like the garland
the buffalo
wears to its slaughter

Anonymous

Fingers
under my skirt
and fumbles—me laughing
squeezing him closer—
strains at
the knot already
untied

Chandra

Twilight
moon crescent
red veil sky—
like crimson
fabric a girl's breast
the love-scratch
just showing
through

Anonymous

First time
pregnant
her friends asking
    Is there
       something you crave?
artless to
glance at her
lover

Gajasinha

The monk
stares at her navel
　　she at his face
　　the moon
begging bowl
ladle
crows snatch
them both away

Shashiraga

Youngest bride
of the hunter
    just a peacock
    feather
    thrust in her braid
struts among her
co-wives
    though they wear
    elephant pearl

Pottisa

Hut of reeds
tendrils
off in the forest
    birds
        scattering
beating their wings
upwards—
young wife at her
housework hears them
arms and legs
suddenly weak

Chaya

Skirt whipped
by wind
away from young thighs—
    a toothmark—
and her old
mother
a glimpse at that
jewel box
    is pleased

Hala

Mother-in-law
sleeps over there
so does the
rest of the household but
   traveler
       this is my bed
       don't trip over
       it in the dark

Anonymous

Between her little
son and her
husband
the lady sits—
        milk leaks
        from one breast
        teased by a fingernail
        the other one
        stiffens

Hala

Falling
 thunderbolt quavers
less than her husband's
 bowstring

 —heard it!
and with her
skirt's edge
is wiping the eyes
of those also
 abducted

Karna

Note: Evidently an entire epic, unknown to us but familiar to the original audience, lies behind this verse.

Water and scraps of meat
she has trained
the dog carefully—
It receives her lover
but bays loudly
when her husband appears
on the road

Anonymous

Day of my period,
turmeric smeared on my cheeks,
he forced
me all over with kisses—
Today I am washed
decked out with elegant jewels
he shrinks
from my touch

Anonymous

If no man
has visited during
the night
why do you stumble on
weak legs all morning
drowsy as a newborn buffalo calf
suckled on
seven day milk——?

Kanteshvara

Mother
with the blink of an eye
his love vanished
A trinket gets
dangled
into your world
you reach out and it's gone

Hala

Girlhood
sweeps past like a river
days are fast travelers
not a single night's ever returned
And still you
cling to this unfathomable
notion
of chastity

Anonymous

House to house
she scours
the dog-infested village for you
One day the curs
will devour that trapped
bird of a girl

Devaraja

Traveler look
the midday sun's fearsome
your shadow huddles under
your body
I've a small
cottage close by if you'd
like to
rest & cool off

Surabhivatsa

Once, Honey-dripper
you took
pleasure from no other flower—
today, old affections
discarded
you pass the white
jasmine heavy
with fruit

Matanga

Today at the wedding
Parvati's bridesmaids saw
a lucky omen—
Siva had uncoiled his serpent
bracelet &
laid it far off

Anuraga

Swept along by the
rising
torrent of water
crow has no thought for her own peril
just to reach the embankment—
her nest her
endangered chicks

Mana

Heart
pierced by the
love-god's
swift arrow she tries
to retain her girlfriend's advice
tries & tries but just
can't

Mana

Hear what I say—
along the Godavari River
an impenetrable
thicket,
in it a *madhuka* tree
sweeps the earth with great blossoms
The seasons
will turn & even those
bright massive branches
will one
day be gone

Mana

Word has it
he's lying
and plans to leave
at daybreak tomorrow—
O Lady Night
engulf us
keep the dawn from us

Nishpata

Lone buck
in the clearing
nearby doe
eyes him with such
longing
that there
in the trees the hunter
seeing his own girl
lets the bow drop

Anonymous

Afterword[1]

You find in the best poems from the Sanskrit a clarity of outline and directness of emotion that recall only a few other poetic traditions. Perhaps *The Greek Anthology*, its tender erotic themes treated with such gestural simplicity, comes closest to the poetry of classical India. Sappho and Meleager, Vidya and Yogeshvara—they might have lived in neighboring villages. Certainly they would have recognized the impulse behind one another's verse. Yet fleet as the Sanskrit poems sound, fifteen centuries having lapsed to dust since their composition, like their Greek counterparts they are the result of a deliberately applied craft.

Sanskrit with its daunting vocabulary and its seemingly endless grammatical possibilities—in which the poet by a subtle gesture can transform virtually any part of speech into some other—is one of the planet's profound monuments.

"It is the Hindus' Pyramid, their Sphynx, their Ziggurat, their Parthenon," wrote the French poet René Daumal in the 1930s. Millennia earlier, grammarians of India had reflected on their language's architectonic arrangement, its labyrinthine ability to enclose meaning within meaning, and could not picture it the output of a solely human labor. They termed their alphabet *deva-nagari*, "city of the gods," and charged their poets with its curatorship. However remote, uncertain, or forbidding the reaches of Sanskrit, the poets of ancient India found ways to visit, and to record their discoveries in verse. The Anglo-Saxon poet who wrote "The Ruin" must have felt some comparable awe when, gazing out over the towns and baths of a long-vanished Roman army, he attributed the massive, wrecked walls to a labor of giants.

Little information about the individual poets of Sanskrit has survived the centuries. Until Europeans arrived on Indian shores with double-entry ledger books and a tradition of historical investigation, Indian scholars had been temperamentally disinclined to record dates, dynasties, dwelling places, or other biographical information about their poets. Those who cared, cared for the poetry. For the rest it was a matter of folklore, fair material for anyone who could make fable vivid enough that storytellers might keep it alive in the popular mind. As a result, Sanskrit poetry drifts in a way curiously detached from history or chronicle. Modern scholars trying to locate some court, or the period in which a particular poet wrote, can do so only against a relative time-scale supplied by the language of the surviving manuscripts.

Classical Sanskrit poetry, or *kavya*, flourished from about 400 C.E. until the Moslem invasions of India in the twelfth and thirteenth centuries. In the north, where Brahmins exerted their strictest influence, men alone learned and spoke Sanskrit, the language of liturgy, science, and poetry. Law or convention restricted women to local tongues, the vernaculars of India's towns and villages. This makes it safe to assume that the women poets lived principally in the south. Most notable and likely the earliest of these women whose work has survived is Vidya, a poet of bold and untamable temper. Today she has no reputation beyond a circle of Sanskrit specialists, and I have included a disproportionate number of her poems because they stand with the best poetry from ancient Greece, China, or Japan. Vidya's peers are Sappho, Li Ch'ing Chao, and Lady Komachi, yet her poems lie scattered through a number of anthologies; no one has bothered to collect them.[2]

The few available facts suggest that most Sanskrit poets attached themselves to royal courts, making their livings as skilled artisans, much the way musicians did, or sculptors, painters, dancers, jugglers. Reliable accounts left by Chinese travelers of the period suggest an enviable age for the arts and sciences. Kings and princes patronized the poets and brought them to court, ennobling themselves through the arts their reigns produced as much as through military exploits or public works. Secularized in the cosmopolitan ambience of these courts, poetic composition still bears the trace of an ancient ritual theater that once combined poetic recitation with music, dance, costume, and scenery, from which it divided off at some point in the remote past. While the separate arts pursued independent directions, common meters for poetry retained names like *the slow stepper, girl wearing a garland,* and *tiger's sport.* It must only have been with reluctance that the poets left off fashioning their rhythms to the step of the dancer's foot.[3]

No one can tell how much of India's poetry has disappeared. Monsoon and desert climates, tropical insects, arrogant local rulers, and intemperate foreigners, all have savaged the manuscripts. Throughout what remains, references crop up to plays and verse-cycles that have not survived the depredations. The poems I have translated are examples of what the anthologies, likening them to gemstones, call *subhashita*—literally, a "well-wrought utterance." Each is a self-sustained verse, composed as such, but many may also be the fragmentary remnant of some all-night theater production or dance-cycle performed under torchlight.[4]

A number of massive anthologies that have surfaced in Himalayan monastic libraries and other remote protected places preserve these fragile isolated poems. Around 1100 C.E. a Bengali Buddhist scholar named Vidyakara compiled his *Subhasitaratnakosa,* or "Treasury of Court Poetry."[5] I've drawn many of my selections from this anthology since it is available in a fine critical edition from Harvard University Press. It is a late collection though, its most vital poetry dating from a period centuries earlier than its compilation. By the time Vidyakara was drafting his anthology the winds of change were upon India.

Separate from the Sanskrit poetry I've selected poems from a manuscript known as *King Hala's Sattasai* (or *Gaha-kosa*). This anthology of seven hundred succinct verses occurs in a literary dialect of ancient Maharashtra State, similar to Sanskrit, and probably predates all but the earliest Sanskrit verse. The poems it preserves give a glimpse of India's classical tradition in germination. They are all regionally specific to a watershed drained by the Godavari River, which winds through the anthology like a presiding goddess, and they differ from the urbane Sanskrit poems in their cultural backdrop—tribal hunting collectives and small agrarian villages. A simpler, less self-conscious milieu, but in *Technicians of the Sacred* Jerome Rothenberg reminds us that "primitive means complex." These ancient Maharashtri poets wrote verse as tight and elaborate as that in any language.

From the time of its codification in the sixth century B.C.E., the Sanskrit language extended across India, gathering into a unified literary tradition an otherwise kaleidoscopic culture which from region to region divides into a bewildering array of customs and dialects. The poetry of India's classical period, from the Gupta Empire in the fourth century C.E., occurred in Sanskrit, the way you could say its representative sculpture occurred in sandstone. Then, eight hundred years ago, displaced Turkish Moslems stormed down from the rugged passes of present-day Afghanistan. In a series of assaults they shattered the splendid amber and ivory courts and laid waste the dignified Buddhist universities, defacing statuary and torching the libraries. Better organized and far hungrier than the resisting forces, they brought under strict control the major cities of the north, as well as the connecting roadways. These soldiers instituted Urdu, their "speech of the camp," as the dominant language, at which point the genius of Indian poetry took to the streets and villages, abandoning the devastated Sanskrit culture and finding haven in India's so-called vernacular tongues.

I first came upon these poems as many arrive at the site of work to be done, by an accident that in retrospect appears unavoidable. In 1973, having saved a bit of money, I climbed aboard a plane to India, carrying a pocket knife and a spare shirt. That was the year of Watergate. It was also the year a flood of particularly virulent drugs overwhelmed our nation's schools. I don't know who was responsible, but they more or less succeeded in neutralizing the protests that would, nonetheless, manage in their aftershocks to bring down the Nixon imperium.

America seemed a dismal and frightening place. The so-called "war at home," which largely pitted youth of the United States against the military-industrial establishment, had subsided; but in Vietnam the "war overseas" stormed on. India, geographically proximate to the most fearsome fighting, culturally proximate to the ravaged citizens of Laos and Cambodia, promised something—I couldn't know what. To say "a handful of poems" makes it sound more trite and absurdly more magisterial than it was. One might as well say "a handful of phantoms." And America or India, what can a man or a woman lay hold of that will prove, over the years, more than a handful of phantoms?

Nearly twenty years later I can't pretend to have located anything. I have picked up Sanskrit where and how I could, tracking the grammar during stopovers at three different universities.[6] Working best when alone I've conferred with scholars only infrequently on questions of interpretation. And I can't claim any singular competence. The language is too complex for any but the most resolute to master; my interests time and again take me elsewhere. Others have broken important ground; I owe an unrepayable debt to those few noteworthy scholars, Daniel Ingalls and Barbara Miller in particular, neither of whom I've ever met, who have worked difficult terrain to familiarize American readers with Sanskrit poetry.[7]

So to the poems. On the surface they have little to do with present-day India as I encountered her in 1973 and again in 1986.[8] In the evenings, crouched over the coals of a small dung fire in the curb, I would smoke *ganja* with wiry thin-armed rickshaw drivers. These men live on the cusp between industrial urban India and the Neolithic villages of their childhood where the old stories and poems still precipitate the common dream. Drawn to the cities for work, their labor is bonecrushing. They pedal their three-wheeled cycles, weighted with two plump middle-class Indians or two tourists, up deceptively graded hills for miles. The sun under which they work will at midsummer heat the shade to 120 degrees. I've been told a driver can expect to live about six or eight years after purchasing his rickshaw. He sleeps in the streets and sends whatever money he makes back to his family village.

What is it that fuels these men? Duty? Courage? Devotion? They collect on street corners or curbstones when night begins to cool things off a bit. There, from their eyes flashing with firelight as they converse heatedly and late into the night over their *ganja*, you gather a ferocious loyalty—to their families, to their caste, to each other—and an equally ferocious nihilism. What has this to do with the ancient poems? More and more I want a poetry that can test its edge against people like this, less and less am I certain how poetry does it.

Two thousand years have passed since someone composed the first of these poems. Religions and rulers have come and gone, caravans and armies sweep past like wind in the night. Already the twentieth century with its wars and unprecedented famines has nearly run to its limit. No, not immortality, but a terrible swift impermanence haunts love and chases poetry out of the dark reaches of human thought. Certain bittersweet delights taken in one another, when in our groping way we manage to touch another person, balance the betrayals and loss. If these translations convey a hint of it they have more than repaid the labor.

—Andrew Schelling
Berkeley, 1990

[1] This is the introduction to *Dropping the Bow* as I wrote it in 1990. I have decided to let it stand as first published, reserving a few reappraisals or updated thoughts for footnotes.

[2] Eight more of Vidya's poems appear in my book *The Cane Groves of Narmada River* (City Lights, 1998).

[3] Poetrty was closely aligned with theater in classical India, but I can no longer see ritual theater as its origin. That is a much later invention, popularized by the *Natya Shastra* (ascribed to Bharata Muni, but probably compiled between 400 B.C.E and 200 C.E., the work of many writers). Ancient ritual theater—or any whole art, like opera—presumes a pretty advanced stage of material civilization. Poetry's roots go deep into the Paleolithic, where a good song would have been part of anyone's medicine bundle.

[4] Another term is *kanda-kavya*, "threshed" or separate poem.

[5] Daniel H.H. Ingalls has translated the full collection as *An Anthology of Sanskrit Court Poetry*, Harvard University Press, 1965. His introduction remains one of the finest and most sympathetic accounts of Sanskrit poetry. Vidyakara's anthology had vanished for nearly a thousand years. In the 1930s it was found in a barn attached to the monastery at Ngor, Tibet—first by the Indian Sanskritist, Rahula Sankrityayana, then by the Italian explorer, art collector, and Buddhist scholar Giuseppe Tucci. Under nearly impossible conditions each managed to photograph the full manuscript and carry the plates back to India. The manuscript, possibly Vidyakara's personal copy, has not been seen again.

[6] My teachers: Rama Sharma (University of Rochester), Jan Willis (U.C. Santa Cruz), and Sally Sutherland Goldman and Vidvan Bhatta (U.C. Berkeley). I want to express my deepest gratitude to each of them, as well as to Padmanabh Jaini (Berkeley) who helped me see that a "career" in Sanskrit would be impossible, freeing me to pursue poetry instead.

[7] Miller died in 1993 and Ingalls in 1999. I never did meet either of them. Ingalls trained a generation of Sanskrit scholars, and his influence goes well beyond his writings. As for Barbara Miller, my estimate of her work has increased steadily over the years. Her critical editions of Bhartrihari and Jayadeva are remarkable. She must have been a fine woman, brave, independent, & profoundly committed to her work. Almost no North American in Sanskrit studies worked with the poetry tradition for decades. The years Miller put into her studies, in India and the United States, comparing manuscripts, seeking out knowledgeable Indian pundits, wrangling over problematic scripts, scrutinizing tattered manuscripts, have given us reliable, readable texts of much of India's indispensable classical

poetry.

8 I have returned to India three times since I wrote this, in 1993, 2007, and 2008. Most recently I was invited to lecture and read poetry in Delhi and in the state of Himachal Pradesh. I was able to discuss India's poetry and music with learned friends: singer Vidya Rao, Sanskrit scholar Raji Ramannan, film-maker Kumar Shahani, poet Prabodh Parikh, and editor and literary scholar Ira Raja.

NOTES ON THE POETS & POEMS

Sanskrit Poets

The AMARUSHATAKA, or "Hundred Poems of Amaru," is a cycle of some of the finest poetry in Sanskrit. The best estimate dates it to the second half of the 8th century. Some Sanskrit copies are illustrated with delicate, occasionally explicit miniature paintings, and there exist four versions with the poems in radically different order. Tradition ascribes the poems to an Amaru or Amaruka, unknown except for his poetry, who is said to have been a king of Kashmir. Western scholars tend to regard Amaru as an anthologist who may have composed some of the poems in his book. I used to think this the case, but after having studied and translated all hundred-odd poems (see my *Erotic Love Poems from India*, Shambhala Publications, 2004), I came to believe it a verse-cycle composed by a single author—though various editors in subsequent centuries rearranged the order of the poems. Frequent use of a specific grammatic form, the locative absolute, seems to me a "signature" of this precise, heartbroken, and psychologically astute poet.

The traditional account from India: the 8th century yogin, ascetic, & philosopher Shankara held a debate with an adept of another spiritual system. Shankara was dominating his rival when the man's wife stepped in. She silenced him with a series of metaphysical questions, put into metaphors of sexual love. Shankara being celibate had no reply. He asked for a hundred nights' recess to examine her questions, then, through powers of yoga, left his body with his disciples. He entered the corpse of a recently deceased king of Kashmir, Amaru, who lay on the pyre awaiting cremation, and Amaru woke to life. For a hundred nights Shankara tasted love in Amaru's harem, each night with a different partner. After the hundredth night had elapsed—he remained a few additional nights, to rest up or to further his studies—he returned to his own sleeping body. Reentering the hall of debate the following day he vanquished his tormentor. Later he committed the poems to writing, signing them "Amaru."

BHAMAHA. Author of the *Alamkara Sastra*, an influential early treatise, in which he examines linguistic technique— metaphor, rhyme, rhythm, figures of speech—as the essence of poetry. His intent, I believe, is to get at the magical qualities of language above and below the threshold of meaning. I read his book as a marvelous grimoire of poetic craft.

BHARTRIHARI. Two figures known as Bhartrihari appear in India. One wrote an important grammar, still highly regarded. The other (some think they were the same man) was a poet. He left three hundred poems—possibly a few more or a few less—thematically arranged in three books of a hundred: Counsel, Romance, and Renunciation. Some scholars have viewed the books as representing three distinct periods in the poets life, but more likely the legends about Bhartrihari get nearer the truth. A courtier or advisor to a king, Bhartrihari vacillated between a scholar's position at court, and the bark-clad forest renunciant's life, going back and forth seven times. During his last stint at court, the poet gave some sort of enchanted amulet to a woman he loved madly. She longed for another man though, and passed the gift on to him. This man desired yet another girl, and made the treasure over to her—who adored Bhartrihari—and completing the terrible cycle offered the amulet back to him. A circle of hopeless desire, painful vanity, crushed love, betrayal. Bhartrihari quit the court and fled to the forests & rivers to meditate on "moon-crested Siva."

Translated into Dutch in 1651, German in 1663, Bhartrihari was the first Sanskrit poet brought to Europe. Barbara Miller has edited and translated all his poems. There is also a translation by Greg Bailey.

BHAVABHUTI. One of India's principle dramatists, active in the early 8th century. He was a brahmin from the southern town of Padmapura. The poem I've included occurs in the play *Uttararamacarita*. When Bhavabhuti had finished writing his play, he rushed to his colleague, Kalidasa, who sat absorbed in a chess game. Bhavabhuti read the manuscript aloud to his friend. Kalidasa never looked away from the chess board. When Bhavabhuti finished, Kalidasa lifted a chess piece, check-mated his opponent, then turned and pronounced the drama perfect—except for one superfluous letter m—in the word *evam*, which occurred in this verse. Bhavabhuti revised the word to *eva* (a widely used term that often carries a subtle gesture more than any specific lexical meaning). The tone became drier, more reserved & at the same time more passionate. It's the understatement that makes the poem so fine in its original. It has been called the most splendid poem in Sanskrit.

BHOJADEVA. Poet, prolific critic, and patron of artists, he was king (Raja) of Dhara from about 1000 to 1055 C.E. He wrote a compendious study of poetry, the *Srngara Prakasa,* which has been edited by V. Raghavan in a critical Sanskrit edition for Harvard University Press. Raghavan has also published a study, *Bhoja's Srngara Prakasa.* King Bhoja constructed on the grounds of his palace at Dhara a remarkable temple to poetry. The temple, I've read, has become a mosque. Its central deity, Vag-devi (Speech Goddess), was removed by the English, and resides, so I've heard, in the British Museum.

DHARMAKIRTI. Very likely the Buddhist Acharya (teacher) and peerless logician of the seventh century. His name is certainly Buddhist. D.D. Kosambi writes that Dharmakirti's verses "have the grace, sparkle, and clarity which one associates with the best" Sanskrit poems. Octavio Paz's I*n Light of India* gives an interesting account of him and his dual allegiances to logic & poetry.

The Dhvanyaloka, or "Light on Poetic Subtlety," is an important theoretic treatment of *rasa*, the essence of Indian poetry. Its author, Anandavardhana, yogin, poet, and philosopher of 9th century Kashmir, is the preeminent theorist on India's poetics, and places *rasa* in a system of mystical linguistics. He illustrates his study of *dhvani* (suggestion or subtlety) with numerous examples, some of them exquisite poems that survive only in his treatise.

GONANDA. I find only a terse note, that he was a Shaivite, a follower of Shiva.

HASTIPAKA. "Elephant driver." His name may be an invention based on the poem since the name doesn't show up anywhere else. The poem is unique in its way, and one can read it as a tender, precise, exactingly realistic portrait of an elephant herd. Archaic India knew that a sympathetic magic linked elephants and rain clouds though—if you want to take this poem a step deeper. In *Myths and Symbols in Indian Art and Civilization*, Zimmer says elephants were once clouds, able to roam the skies at will. After an angry ascetic "grounded" them (you can look up the story), humans used elephants to lure their old kin, the monsoon storm clouds. When a kingdom suffered drought, a ceremonial elephant was brought to court—sometimes the gift of a neighboring ruler—to draw down rain. With this in mind, the poem could derive from Paleolithic traditions in which shamans exerted control over the weather. The Pueblo Indians of the American Southwest have made a social ritual or community dance of this effort to bring rain. In old India, spoken formulas seem to have been the core of magical tradition, so spells & symbols would have been used. The "poet" resembles a skilled hunter who has no need for a decoy; he only needs to produce the animal's call or an image in words. Here, to capture in magic syllables the fertile presence of an elephant herd, and by this to bring the thunderclouds.

KALIDASA. Surely the most renowned poet and playwright of classical India. He may have lived in the 4th century. Author of many plays and poem-cycles, including *Sakuntala*, which influenced Goethe's *Faust*. Both the poems I have translated are drawn from his *Megadhuta* or *Cloud Messenger*.

Kalidasa was reputedly the favorite poet of a King Kumaradasa, who wrote on the wall of his palace this half verse—

> "A lotus grows on a lotus"
> spoken of, but who's seen it—?

The king offered a reward to whoever best completed the poem. Kalidasa added,

> Two blue water-flowers, your eyes, lady,
> bloom from a white water-lotus.

In the original Sanskrit it is a precise poem (ethnobotany:

dozens of varieties of lotus in India, two named here: the *indivaram*, a small blue flower, and the *ambhoja* or "water born," the white). A courtesan of Kumaradasa's retinue, however, greedy for treasure, poisons Kalidasa (maybe she paints her nipples with arsenic) and offers the verse as her own. Kumaradasa cannot be gulled. Intimate with Kalidasa's style, he recognizes the hand of his poet. He punishes the courtesan, then burns himself in grief on Kalidasa's funeral pyre.

MURARI. Poet and playwright of the Brahmin caste. His dates and place of residence are controversial. Some think he was a Kashmiri of the middle 9th century, others that he lived at the court of "some Kalacuri king," at Mahishmati, on the Narmada River.

PATANJALI. Perhaps the same person who wrote the *Yoga Sutras*. There is also an important grammarian of this name.

RAJASEKHARA. Prolific poet, playwright, and author of *Kavya-Mimamsa*, a well known handbook for poets. Late 9th century, or possibly first quarter of the 10th. His work shows up in all the major anthologies.

SHILABHATTARIKA. Perhaps 9th century. Her poem, *yau kaumaraharah*, "The man who first / took my flower," is to my mind one of the finest lyrics in Sanskrit. It appears in virtually every important anthology. (It has two versions—I've translated the other in *The Cane Groves of Narmada River*, City

Lights, 1997.) Only six poems show up with her name. One is a brief collaborative verse credited in one anthology to her and King Bhoja (Bhojadeva). Perhaps Shila held a position at Bhoja's court. This would place her in the 11th century. As with many of India's early poets, there's nothing conclusive. I hope more of her poems turn up one day.

UTPALARAJA. Numerous Utpalarajas appear in the annals of Kashmir. Nobody knows if one of them was the poet.

VACASPATI. Seven poems attributed to him appear in the anthology *Subhasita-ratna-kosa.* I can't find anything about him.

VAGURA. Abhinanda, a later poet than Vagura, of perhaps the late 9th century, wrote: *nisnatah kavikunjarendracarite marge giram vagurah.* "Vagura is skilled in the path of Language, walked by early master poets." The path is *marga,* a way or trail, originally a deer or wild animal track. Interestingly, a *vagura* is a trap or snare, a *vagurika* a hunter. D.D. Kosambi says the term *vagura* can refer to a writer.

VAKKUTA. Certainly lived after the 9th century. One of his poems laments the passing of the great craftsmen of that period. "Gone is Shrichandra, gone Abhinanda." "Voice, be silent! Why weep? Where is there anyone left to honor you?"

VARAHAMIHIRA. A renowned astronomer, and author of a significant astrological treatise, the *Brhatsamhita.* Probably 6th century. D.D. Kosambi thinks his name odd—it links the "boar" and the "sun"—and he may have been foreign. Possibly Greek or Chinese?

VIDYA (or VIJJAKA). All agree that Vidya is the earliest and the finest of Sanskrit women poets, known for about thirty brief lyrics. She may have lived as early as the 7th century. In one poem she calls herself "dark as the blue lotus petal," tempting one to think she lived to the South where on the whole the complexions are darker and skin tone can appear blue. Rajashekhara, much later, called her the "Kanarese Saraswati" (Saraswati: goddess of verse-craft; Kanara: district in South India). She wrote freely and convincingly of love outside the conventions of marriage, with a uniquely tender good humor. Her thirty poems convince me she wrote love lyrics of the highest quality. See my book *The Cane Groves of Narmada River* for some of her others. A Western scholar once called her "the Sappho of India."

VISHVANATHA. Author of the *Sahityadarpana*, or Mirror of Writing, one of the important poetic handbooks. It is dated about 1350 C.E. I have used Vishvanatha's opening verse, a poem of invocation, as my epigram. In a post-structuralist age, which frequently views language as a poorly fashioned tool, or even a prison house, I find heartening Vishvanatha's belief that Giram Devi, Goddess Language, has power to remove the heart's ignorance, and to "cast into light" the nature of things.

YOGESHVARA. Bengali; active ca. 850-900. The scholar Daniel H.H. Ingalls noted a tendency among poets of Bengal to write a "poetry of village and field." Yogeshvara, chief of these Bengali poets, often looks to rural lifeways for his subject. He took an active, almost anthropological interest in tribal peoples. In this way his poems point to an earlier era. But they also point forward to contemporary concerns: nature literacy, ethnopoetics, and a recovery of the Old Ways. In one poem he states, "My heart belongs to the meadow at the bend in the river."

NOTE ON THE POETS
OF KING HALA'S SATTASAI OR GAHA-KOSA

Hala's anthology of 700 poems predates any Sanskrit collection by several centuries. Estimates for its compilation range from about 200 B.C.E. to 200 C.E. Its poems occur in an old literary *Prakrit* or vernacular of Maharashtra State. The two titles, *Sattasai* (*Seven Hundred*) and *Gaha-kosa* (*Book of Songs*), probably came somewhat later. Forty of the poems have Hala's name attached, but these include a closing verse for each of the book's seven sections: "Here ends the first hundred poems in Hala's book," &c.

Hala was a local warlord or ruler of the Satavahana Dynasty, the same people who painted the exquisite Buddhist murals in the Ajanta Caves. For Hala's sensibility, though, you can't study the bodhisattvas and monks of those paintings. You have to search for the little vignettes of life off at the side, in the gallery shadows—the frequent portraits of lovers. The *Gaha-kosa* is resolutely secular. Aside from his book, nothing certain is known of Hala, though the Godavari River winds through with such a physical presence I regard his collection as a gathering of watershed poems.

The anthology divides the 700 poems into seven chapters, a hundred poems each, and includes names of 278 poets. Nearly half the collection is anonymous. Of the poets named, six or seven or eight are women. Perhaps the anonymous lyrics were composed by women too. The poets' names come from a range of castes and include artisans or workmen—blacksmiths and potters—unlike the later Sanskrit poets who form a professional guild drawn from the "twice-born," educated classes. Since all 700 poems are in the same meter—measured in syllabic weights or *matrakas*, approximately thirty-two syllables per poem—to regard them as based in folk song is probably right. I'd speculate that the poets had ways of reciting or performing them—using drawn out syllables, repeated lines, musical or non-sense syllable insertions—similar to the chanting style of Japanese haiku, or Native American song.

The poems anyhow conjure a period earlier or at least less culturally developed than the Sanskrit—far closer to a lifestyle at the advent of agriculture, when the hunter's bow was still a magical item, and possession of elephant pearl (ivory) suggested true bravery. I have placed these poems after the Sanskrit poems. Why? To suggest a postmodern look towards the Old Ways. The humans who populate the poems come from a village culture, based on agriculture, with tribes in the near hills who still live by hunting. A bit of rustling, low-key warfare, or marauding, seems an unsurprising feature. Of enormous interest: familiarity with nature is specific—plants, animals, geomorphology, eco-zones. The poems show surprisingly little interest in the supernatural though. Dream, vision, spirits, magic spells, rituals for the dead, of these there appear few traces. The poems are almost all about love. Perhaps that's all the magic one needs. Hala wrote the following, and inserted it as one of the first entries to his *Book of Songs*—

> You'd think
> from their
> talk they were adepts
> at love
> Yet they never read
> never even listen
> to deathless
> Prakrit poetry

Bibliography

Amarusatakam. Edited by C.R. Devadhar. Motilal Banarsidass: Delhi, 1959.

Anandavardhana. *Dhvanyaloka.* Critically edited with Introduction, translation, and notes by Dr. K. Krishnamoorthy. Motilal Banarsidass: Delhi, 1974.

Kalidasa. *The Meghaduta.* Narayana Balakrishnan Godabole, ed. Nirnaya-Sagara Press: Bombay, 1911.

Bhartrihari: Poems. Barbara Stoller Miller. Columbia University Press: New York, 1967.

The Prakrit Gatha-Saptasati. Compiled by Satavahana King Hala. Radhagovinda Basak, ed. The Asiatic Society: Calcutta, 1971.

Sahityadarpana by Visvanatha Kaviraja. Annotated with Introduction and Explanatory Commentaries by Mahamahopadhyaya Pandit Durgaprasada Dviveda. Pandurang Jawaji, Proprietor of the Nirnaya-Sagar Press: Bombay, 1936.

Srngaratilakam of Sri Kalidasa. Dr. Kapil Dev Giri. Second edition. Chaukhamba Orientalia: Varanasi, 1985.

Subhasitaratnakosa. Compiled by Vidyakara. Edited by D.D. Kosambi and V.V. Gokhale. Harvard University Press: Boston, 1957.

COMPANIONS FOR THE JOURNEY SERIES

Inspirational work by well-known writers in a small-book format
designed to be carried along on your journey through life.

Volume 14
White Crane
Love Songs of the Sixth Dalai Lama
Translated by Geoffrey R. Waters
1-893996-82-4   86 pages $14.00

Volume 13
Haiku Master Buson
Translated by Edith Shiffert and Yuki Sawa
1-893996-81-6   256 pages $16.00

Volume 12
The Shape of Light
Prose Pieces by James Wright
1-893996-85-9   96 pages $14.00

Volume 11
Simmering Away: Songs from the Kanginshu
Translated by Yasuhiko Moriguchi and David Jenkins
Illustrations by Michael Hofmann
1-893996-49-2   70 pages $14.00

Volume 10
Because of the Rain: Korean Zen Poems
Translated by Won-Chung Kim and Christopher Merrill

1-893996-44-1   96 pages $14.00

Volume 9
Pilgrim of the Clouds
Poems and Essays from Ming Dynasty China
Translated by Jonathan Chaves
1-893996-39-5   192 pages $15.00

Volume 8
The Unswept Path: Contemporary American Haiku
Edited by John Brandi and Dennis Maloney
1-893996-38-7   220 pages $15.00

Volume 7
Lotus Moon: The Poetry of Rengetsu
Translated by John Stevens
Afterword by Bonnie Myotai Treace
1-893996-36-0   132 pages $14.00

Volume 6
A Zen Forest: Zen Sayings
Translated by Soiku Shigematsu
Preface by Gary Snyder
1-893996-30-1   120 pages $14.00

Volume 5
Back Roads to Far Towns: Basho's Travel Journal
Translated by Cid Corman
1-893996-31-X   94 pages $13.00

Volume 4
Heaven My Blanket, Earth My Pillow
Poems from Sung Dynasty China by Yang Wan-Li
Translated by Jonathan Chaves
1-893996-29-8   128 pages $14.00

Volume 3
10,000 Dawns: The Love Poems of Claire and Yvan Goll
Translated by Thomas Rain Crowe and Nan Watkins
1-893996-27-1   88 pages $13.00

Volume 2
There Is No Road: Proverbs by Antonio Machado
Translated by Mary G. Berg & Dennis Maloney
1-893996-66-2   118 pages $14.00

Volume 1
Wild Ways: Zen Poems of Ikkyu
Translated by John Stevens
1-893996-65-4   152 pages $14.00